W9-BII-394

WHOSE POO?

POO ON THE SAVANNA

by

Emilie Dufresne

BEARPORT
PUBLISHING

Minneapolis, Minnesota

Credits:
All images are courtesy of Shutterstock.com, unless otherwise specified. With thanks to Getty Images, Thinkstock Photo, and iStockphoto.

Front Cover - PremiumVector, ainahart, Svietlieisha Olena, Iterum, Yev0, Iron 2016, Valeri Hadeev. Title typeface used throughout - PremiumVector. 2 - STUDIO 11. 4 - Elina Litovkina, robuart. 5 - toowaret. 6&7 - BigBoom. 6 - lukpedclub. 7 - Anan Kaewkhammul, Eric Isselee, Iakov Filimonov. 8 - Sergey Uryadnikov. 9 - Mogens Trolle, vectortatu. 10&11 - John Ceulemans. 11 - a_v_d, Eric Isselee, Iakov Filimonov. 12 - J. NATAYO. 13 - Marie Lemerle, GraphicsRF. 14&15 - TaTum2003, Shanvood. 15 - Anan Kaewkhammul, John Kasawa, Susan Schmitz. 16 - dirkr, Ekaterina_Mikhaylova. 17 - robuart, David Gallaher. 18&19 - KAMONRAT. 19 - Eric Isselee, Iakov Filimonov, Valdis Skudre. 20 - Aspen Photo, puaypuay. 21 - This Is Me, passengerz, MaryValery. 22 - Cristina Romero Palma, Neil Bromhall. 23 - FJAH.

Library of Congress Cataloging-in-Publication Data

Names: Dufresne, Emilie, author.
Title: Poo on the savanna / by Emilie Dufresne.
Description: Fusion. | Minneapolis, Minnesota : Bearport Publishing, [2021]
  | Series: Whose poo? | Includes bibliographical references and index.
Identifiers: LCCN 2020009339 (print) | LCCN 2020009340 (ebook) | ISBN
  9781647473860 (library binding) | ISBN 9781647473914 (paperback) | ISBN
  9781647473969 (ebook)
Subjects: LCSH: Savannas–Juvenile literature. | Feces–Juvenile
  literature.
Classification: LCC QH87.7 .D84 2021 (print) | LCC QH87.7 (ebook) | DDC
  577.4/8–dc23
LC record available at https://lccn.loc.gov/2020009339
LC ebook record available at https://lccn.loc.gov/2020009340

For more information, write to Bearport Publishing, 5357 Penn Avenue South, Minneapolis, MN 55419. Printed in the United States of America.

CONTENTS

ALL ABOUT POO

You do it. Your teacher does it. Even the worms in the ground do it. Everybody poos! But have you ever seen poo and wondered who did it?

Let's look around the savanna and see whose poo we can find.

Don't touch any poo you find on the savanna. Poo has lots of nasty things in it!

On the next pages, you will see poo found on the savanna. Learn about the poo, and then choose which of the three animals you think made the mess!

STAY AWAY SPRAY

What's that lumpy cloud in the water? Is it . . . poo?

This poo is sprayed widely across the land and water.

The poo is a green-brown color. This animal probably eats a lot of plants.

Whose poo could this be? Choose which of these three animals you think did this.

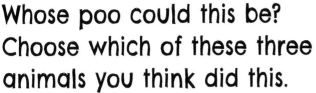

Zebra

How could I even make a poo shower?

If we found the poo in and near the water, this animal probably lives nearby.

Hippopotamus

The poo has bits of grass in it.

Hyena

WHOSE POO WAS IT?

It was the hippopotamus's POO!

It was me! Stand back, I can feel another one coming.

Hippos spend a lot of the hot day in the water to keep cool. They even poo there!

8

Male hippopotamuses use their tails like a **propeller** to fling their poo far. This helps them mark their **territory**.

Hippo poo can kill the fish in the water.

SPLATTER ZONE

WHITE AND CHALKY

Wow—I've never seen a poo like that!

There are lots of poos left in one mound. This is probably a shared toilet.

The white color means there is a lot of calcium in the poo.

Whose poo could this be? Choose which of these three animals you think did this.

Hyena

Because it's a shared toilet, the animal probably lives in a **pack**.

Are you looking at me?

Aardvark

This bright white poo really stands out on the grassy savanna.

You think I did *what*?

Giraffe

WHOSE POO WAS IT?

It was the **hyena's POO!**

Hey! It wasn't just me. The whole pack pooed there.

Hyenas eat animals that they kill or find already dead.

12

MIGHTY MOUNDS

What a mighty poo we have here!

Gross! There are insects eating the poo.

This poo has a lot of grass in it. This animal is probably a plant-eater.

Whose poo could this be? Choose which of these three animals you think did this.

I wish my poo looked like that!

Ostrich

This poo is really big. It must come from a large animal.

Crocodile

There are a lot of pieces of plants in this poo. This animal doesn't digest its food very well.

Elephant

WHOSE POO WAS IT?

It was the **elephant's POO!**

It was me! I made the mound of poo!

An elephant spends about 15 hours a day eating over 300 pounds (136 kg) of food! That's the same as 10 bales of hay!

Elephants may eat a lot, but they don't digest food very well. About half of what they eat goes through them undigested.

An elephant's poo still has lots of good things in it that other animals can eat.

Baby elephants eat their mother's poo to get important bacteria in their bodies.

Thanks, Mom!

17

DOZENS OF DROPS

Look at this pretty pile of droppings! Whose poo could it be?

The poo is very smooth and full of chewed-up plants.

The droppings are the size of grapes. They are squished flat on one side.

WHOSE POO WAS IT?

It was the **giraffe's** **POO!**

I spend about 20 hours of my day eating leaves. You'd poop a lot, too!

Giraffes have tongues that are 1.5 feet (0.5 m) long. That's about the length of a cat. Their tongues help them reach the tallest leaves on the trees.

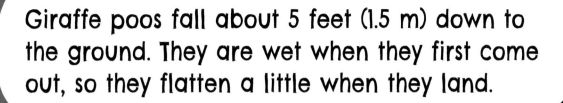

Giraffe poos fall about 5 feet (1.5 m) down to the ground. They are wet when they first come out, so they flatten a little when they land.

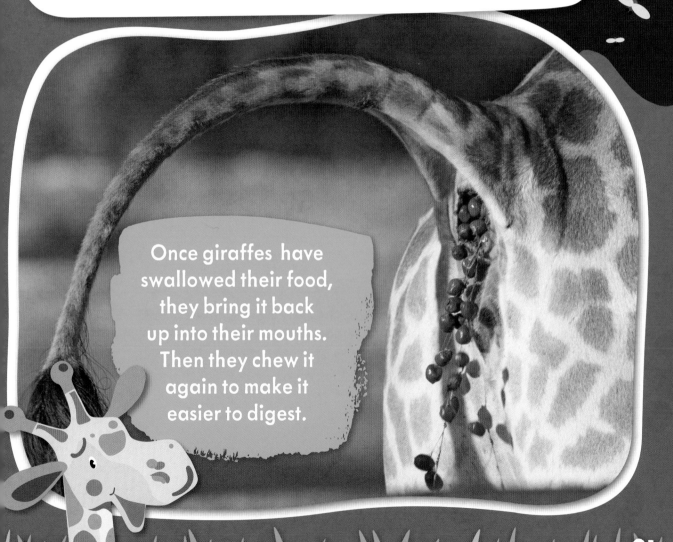

Once giraffes have swallowed their food, they bring it back up into their mouths. Then they chew it again to make it easier to digest.

BONUS POO!

Dung beetles roll other animals' poo to their homes to lay their eggs in. When their eggs hatch, the baby beetles eat the poo.

The kids will love this treat!

A dung beetle can roll a ball that is more than twice its height!

22

POOING IN YOUR PANTS

Vultures will poo and pee all over their own legs. This might sound disgusting and dirty, but their waste helps to kill any nasty bacteria they might have stepped in.

Pooing and peeing on themselves also keep vultures cool on the hot savanna.

I'm out of soap. Can someone poo on me?

GLOSSARY

bacteria tiny living things that live inside animals

calcium something that is in teeth, bones, and shells that makes these things hard and strong

digest to break down food into things that can be used by the body

pack a group of the same animal

prey animals that are eaten by other animals

propeller a device that spins with blades like a fan

savanna a large area of flat land with grass and very few trees

territory the area where an animal lives and finds its food

INDEX

24